STEVE JOBS
LEARN FROM THE
MASTERS

Carl Preston

THE STEVE JOBS WAY

What will you exactly get on this book?

- Quotes from Steve jobs and the course of action for you to follow to equal his success around his own advice and experience.

- What he did and what that particular quote meant to him?

- An answer to the question: How did he do it? How did he deal with the issue? For each quote.

- What can you learn from what he did?

- Why is it likely to be holding you back and not follow his winner advice. Tips to avoid this and become successful.

- Resources and further learning to build up your plan of action towards tackling every issue and open your way towards success.

Quotes to understand what it gets to becoming Steve Jobs and awakening the entrepreneur within you.

Are you trying to find the best way to motivate and inspire yourself in life, but aren't quite sure where to start? Then one of the most comfortably assertive ways to start changing your life is to start building a long-term plan using the ideas and ideals of other people from across time and history.

Learn how Steve Jobs character and mentality made him become the genius he was.

In this guide, you will find a list of excellent quotes from the imperious Steve Jobs, the brains behind Apple.

People like Steve Jobs should be greatly respected as they bring so much to the table in terms of innovation and learning, and can be a source of information and advice for everyone out there who feels like they need this input and inspiration in their lives.

Through this guide, tanks to Steve Jobs tips and quotes readers shall be able to:

- Learning from Steve Jobs some critical concepts about entrepreneurial life and personal growth.

- Find a way to understand Steve Jobs quotes and put them into a context that fits the parallels of their own life.

- Create a long-term plan that will ensure they can change what is holding them back using the information and Steve Jobs advice that's provided within.

This can act as your guidebook to success and prosperity, giving you the access that you need to truly understanding what makes people like Steve Jobs the inspirations they are. and how you can use what they knew to create a stronger and more responsive future for yourself and others.

The power lies in your hands, the advice is in this book.

Do it the Steve Jobs way!

"He made it, therefore you can do it"

Aer you interested in finding out what the world of Steve Jobs was like? Then you are in the right place. This guide will help you understand some of his most notable quotes, as well as how you can implement them into your own life.

They should help you see a different side to the statement itself outside of the wisdom that it holds, and this makes a massive difference to your capabilities and your chances of actually getting through the job unimpeded.

The great work and commitment that people like Jobs can put forward to the success they achieved can be the ultimate springboard for anyone to learn from regardless of their placing or their position.

Whether you are looking for help and inspiration in your personal or professional life you should find that the details held within this book make the perfect set of solutions to follow on with.

By doing so, you greatly increase your chances of seeing long-term success whilst growing and developing a personality and an ambition that is bound to create a much easier future for yourself as you start to move forward in your life.

Indeed, with this eBook, you should finally be able to understand some of the most pertinent parts of business and life in general, as well as how to make your personal ambitions fuel your professional ones.

The quotes in here are incisive, interesting and will give you plenty of time to pause for thought – so let's start!

Content

Quote #1 1

Quote #2 4

Quote #3 7

Quote #4 10

Quote #5 13

Quote #6 16

Quote #7 19

Quote #8 22

Quote #1

"Innovation distinguishes between a leader and a follower."

What did Jobs mean by this?

Basically, the easiest way to break this quote down would be to look at it as saying that those who just follow the process set for them are always bound to be just a subordinate, someone in the background. However, if you are capable of really joining in with the ideology of the group you are likely to also just be a follower. What makes someone a leader is that they can break protocol and still have people listening to their ideas.

By inventing something new that eventually becomes workplace protocol, or achieving something similar, you set out your opportunity to really start driving forward and creating something far more enjoyable than it may have once been – this really does make a big difference. Someone who innovates can get by being disliked – look at Jobs himself – so long as you bring something fresh to work.

What did he do about it?

Given that Jobs was probably the worst possible example of what a textbook described as "a leader" he is one of the most important people to listen to about this. He never got on well with his staff and was poor at communicating, but he brought a huge amount of influence to the table – people may have hated his approach, but they loved his results.

He was so good at what he wanted to do in life, that he influenced people regardless of their personal opinion on him. Someone who isn't scared about breaking protocol and making people follow their lead is far more likely to get the respect that they are looking for.

Why are you not doing this today?

The main reason most don't try and innovate themselves is a fear of being exposed by their seniors. If someone does not like what you do and is not a fan of the job that you put forward, then they are not particularly interested in you if you just follow protocol. However, this is the perception most people have; they stay within the set boundaries as they know that they don't fit in perfectly with the group themselves.

Instead of this deliberately painful and challenging process, you can put yourself in a much better position if you lose the fear of making change. Be the one who instigates a new position and you might find that personal differences are put aside due to respect for your craft and your talent.

What can be learned from this?

Don't always worry about following convention – if you are good at what you do then you should never be afraid of breaking protocol to innovate. The best leaders take risks and make new protocol instead of always being hamstrung by the inevitability of red tape in the workplace. If you know your role and your job then you can easily take full control and make things go the way that you wanted.

Innovating is far more important than just following with the orders given – this will help you define yourself further away from being just another face within the group.

Resources to change for better

http://www.inc.com/the-muse/4-simple-ways-to-become-more-innovative.html

https://www.americanexpress.com/us/small-business/openforum/articles/7-ways-to-outsmart-your-brains-wiringand-become-more-innovative/

http://www.forbes.com/sites/groupthink/2013/10/15/5-ways-to-be-more-innovative-in-the-digital-age/

Quote #2

"I'm convinced that about half of what separates successful entrepreneurs from the non-successful ones is pure perseverance."

What did Jobs mean by this?

A man of many words and quotes, Jobs refers to here that the idea of being a successful entrepreneur is all about being able to put up with the mistakes and the problems.

The amazing inventions and ideas on the market today never just magically worked or came together out of nowhere; they were the subject of hours of failure, frustration, anger, upset and bewilderment at why they never worked!

The difference, though, is that the top entrepreneurs in the world – the people like Steve Jobs that we have heard of – have been capable of making that kind of progressive change.

If they don't mind putting the effort in and working through problems, willing to persevere and show mental fortitude, then anything can be possible.

What did he do about it?

Always stayed motivated, and never gave up. Look at where Apple got to in his tenure – and look at how his relationship with others was at the time. His colleagues hated him for the most part, and he hated them.

He couldn't make sense to most people and was seen as being too hard to work with – but the results he found were incredible. This is because Jobs literally made himself a living out of never giving up and never backing down.

If something was too hard to program, he found a way. If there was no logical or logistical way to put something together he would find a way. The man had incredible mental fortitude and this is what set him apart from others.

Why are you not doing this today?

It's very hard to look at life this way but if you don't you really have to. Life is all about persevering and putting up with problems that may seem just beyond you at this moment in time – if you don't give up, though, you have a chance of becoming the success that you always dreamt of.

Many entrepreneurs will need to get through the hardest days on nothing but personal motivation and a belief that what they have to offer needs to be seen by the world.

If you cannot do this then being an entrepreneur is not for you – the success stories out there all came through failure and used it as an energy to ignite their efforts and propel them towards success.

What can be learned from this?

The easiest lesson to take away from this is that Steve Jobs never gave up – and nor should you. The man had huge problems with communication and with social workings around other people, but it did not matter one bit as he created one of the most powerful empires on the planet through never giving up.

Apple was finished to start with – and now, it's one of the most powerful companies in modern history.

They were established through the sheer force of will and control of ability that Jobs had, ensuring that when he kept working others always would. Whether it's your business or your marriage, everything that you work upon in life that needs innovation also needs an indomitable will that cannot be broken.

Resources to change for better

http://shakeoffthegrind.com/extraordinary-goals/12-experts-share-overcome-failure-discouragment

http://blog.uncollege.org/overcoming-failure-the-pereseverance-of-henry-ford

http://www.highspeedlowdrag.org/persevere-in-failure/

Quote #3

"For the past 33 years, I have looked in the mirror every morning and asked myself: 'If today were the last day of my life, would I want to do what I am about to do today?'

And whenever the answer has been 'No' for too many days in a row, I know I need to change something."

What did Jobs mean by this?

This is a brilliant quote which succinctly sums up the man's prowess and his abilities. If you spend too much of your time looking at doing things you aren't sure about – in life or business – then you need to force change somewhere along the line.

All of those things that occur because of emotions like fear and embarrassment will mean nothing when you are no longer here, so it's much easier for you to start understanding how to force positive change in your life.

The fact that you will be heading to the grave one day means that you need to start that realizing that the legacy you leave behind is more important than anything. If your legacy is behind hampered by inactivity or unproductiveness, it's time to change things.

What did he do about it?

Well, the man himself was using the quote to discuss the fact he was given a short time to live due to a form of cancer that was more or less incurable. Or so he thought. It made him really look at death in a more acute manner, but after some biopsy tests he found out he was going to be fine; however, it was that acute interaction with death that made him "suck it up" and start thinking of himself in a more considered manner.

By finally deciding to start making changes in his life without worrying about what others would think or anything of the sort, he made it easier to force change – looking at life like he was about to die was actually a pretty smart move!

Why are you not doing this today?

Most of us are caught up in the fear that what we do will be dissected and looked at by others negatively. If you look at what you are achieving in life at the moment and feel like it's not what you were hoping to achieve then your only real way out of that problem is to start building a long-term plan to fix this. The reason most of us don't do what Jobs said, though, and ask ourselves this question is because we feel we don't have the time.

We go with what seems to be the only option, but without asking ourselves tough questions it's impossible to know if that question really works. Always make sure you push yourself on the boundaries and these limits within your mind, as it's vital to ensuring you embrace the decisions you make.

What can be learned from this?

The most important detail that you can take from this quote, I think, is that it's important to question yourself more often. We can find ourselves just going with protocol because it sounds good or because someone else followed this path – but what path suits you? Where do you want to start heading in life?

If you wish to learn from this quote then you need to realize that, with just a bit of brief discussion inside the mind, you can see where you are going wrong and – crucially – how to avoid this problem from unfolding in the future.

Resources to change for better

http://www.fengshuidana.com/2014/08/12/10-ways-to-know-for-sure-that-it-is-time-to-make-a-big-change-in-your-life/

http://liveboldandbloom.com/06/lifestyle/are-you-ready-to-change-your-life-10-ways-to-know-for-sure

http://lynnrobinson.com/4-ways-to-know-its-time-to-change-your-life/

Quote #4

"Remembering that you are going to die is the best way I know to avoid the trap of thinking you have something to lose. You are already naked. There is no reason not to follow your heart"

What did Jobs mean by this?

This is one of his most philosophical quotes and therefore one of the hardest to break down – the main trap that people walk into, though, is living their life to the expectations of others rather than themselves.

When you take a risk in life – personally or professionally – you are putting your head above the parapet and hoping for the best. What most people do, though, is they only put their head half out as they are scared of losing what they have through taking too much of a risk.

However, what we desire in our lives is all about being able to leave a legacy and the fact we feel embarrassed/upset/nervous etc. should only be a tiny problem for the day. When we pass, it no longer matters – what matters is what you left behind for others to enjoy.

What did he do about it?

Well, Steve Jobs is sadly no longer with us but he made sure he lived his life to this very mentality and philosophy.

Look at what he left behind; a technical juggernaut that will continue to set trends, and make trends, within the tech industry for years to come ensuring that his legacy will never be lost or left behind in any way, shape or form. Since we all start with nothing in life anyway, and you are left with nothing when you die, he went full throttle to ensure that his dreams were met.

The quote sums up his personality perfectly – and it's something everyone could learn from in life.

Why are you not doing this today?

The fear of failure or of embarrassment, reputational damage etc. is something that holds everyone back and if you do this yourself it's easy to see why your success is limited. However, if you can push forward in life and start working towards actually doing this – forgetting about the consequence and only looking at what the end benefit could be for yourself – then you are going to massively benefit in the future.

Everyone can benefit from using this kind of intelligent thinking in their lives and when you start to push for the depth and the change that thinking like this can bring on, it makes an incredible difference as you are less likely to find yourself hampered by believing that you will lose out.

What can be learned from this?

Basically, stop leaving your life in fear of loss! Instead live your life with the possibility of gain. If you take "the plunge" and cost yourself a lot of money, so what? Did you help other people out by doing this? Yeah, you did! Now others that you love in your life can get the help that they need. They can be left with a proper legacy through your hard work and your endeavors.

Even in normal life – going into a relationship, taking a risk, buying a house, anything at all – you should never be held back by the "what if" or the potential problems which can be caused by that.

No, you should be spending your time worrying about how you'll maximize your opportunities!

Resources to change for better

http://www.purposefairy.com/65969/how-to-listen-to-your-heart-even-if-your-mind-disagrees/

http://www.mindbodygreen.com/0-13187/5-reasons-to-follow-your-heart.html

http://conniechapman.com/finding-the-courage-to-follow-your-heart/

Quote #5

"Your work is going to fill a large part of your life, and the only way to be truly satisfied is to do what you believe is great work. And the only way to do great work is to love what you do. If you haven't found it yet, keep looking. Don't settle."

What did Jobs mean by this?

If you look around at your life – your friends, family, colleagues etc. – and then you will notice that just about everyone you talk to hates their job. Everyone hates the idea of working all those hours just to get nothing back in return or to never be involved within the overall creative process.

Most people are disengaged from what they do as they feel it does not connect with their style or their personality, but this comes from one of two things; not knowing what they are passionate about, or being unable to work with what they feel the most caring about.

The quote is about enabling people to move on from a dead-end job they hate "because it pays well". Ambition and accomplishment trumps finance.

What did he do about it?

Well, look at Apple! The guy himself never stuck into an office clerk job or something similar and instead pushed himself into something a bit more ambitious (the whole Apple thing seems to have really taken off!).

This is what it's all about – never settling into something you only kind of enjoy, or more importantly settling into something you don't like. You can make money in other ways in life but it's more important to be happy.

When you love your job and feel like it matches your virtues in life you are so much more likely to keep at it, and to actually make it work in your favor.

Why are you not doing this today?

So, what are you doing to make this happen? If you are in a job your dislike then you are probably in it because of the money. It's time to make this stop – you should start immediately looking for a new job, as nothing is worse in life than just settling.

You would never settle in a second class relationship or marriage, so why a career?

What can be learned from this?

The main thing that can be learned from this quote is quite simple – just taking what you are given in life is a ridiculous concept.

You should always fight to be distinguished and to feel happy with the choices that you make in life. Why should you stay in something you hate just because it gives you a bit of money?

It's better to build up towards a long-term legacy of ambition than just stick in a job for a wage. Wages will come if you are successful, and success is made possible if you really care about your job.

Resources to change for better

http://www.mycareerquizzes.com/career-test

http://www.forbes.com/sites/louisefron/2014/11/14/three-steps-for-finding-your-perfect-job-career-and-life/

http://www.theguardian.com/careers/careers-blog/find-your-ideal-career

Quote #6

"Sometimes when you innovate, you make mistakes. It is best to admit them quickly, and get on with improving your other innovations."

What did Jobs mean by this?

It's easy to be hubristic when you come up with an idea, and never admit that you got it wrong. However, this just puts other people in a tight spot as you will soon find yourself having to defend your ideas – that don't work – from too many people. If you are innovating in life or in business you need to be prepared to admit when your innovations have gone wrong and actually put you in trouble instead of helping you get out of it.

By doing so you make it easier to correct change instead of going until it's too late.

What did he do about it?

Well, look at the amount of problems Apple have had with their own software when innovating. The likes of the iPod, iPad and iPhone have all had major technical glitches as time has gone on but the company dealt with them, and Jobs wasn't egotistical enough to deny his failures. His ego allowed him to take command and make these things happen but he was humble enough to realize when things weren't going to plan.

This is the mark of a good man and someone who can be trusted, as he corrected mistakes to help solve other problems.

Why are you not doing this today?

If you someone who innovates a lot, how often do you take the critique that comes your way? Do you accept that critique or do you get offended by it? It really does come down to how you handle this information coming at you; are you capable of just ignoring it and moving on with your life?

Or do you feel like the critique on you is a genuinely personal attack, aimed at belittling your achievements and holding you back in some capacity?

If you are not changing innovations because they were your innovations, you need to look closely.

What can be learned from this?

Never be arrogant enough to think that only you have the answers when you innovate. It may be your idea but it's also your mistake that holds it back from being a true success; always take the time needed to work on this and make sure the plan can be put in place as soon as you possibly need it to be.

It's better to admit your failings than hold everyone else back on the account of them – never be the person who creates an idea but then also holds it back by failing to adjust or admit your failings.

Resources to change for better

http://www.lifehack.org/articles/work/how-to-admit-your-mistakes.html

http://www.forbes.com/sites/amyanderson/2013/05/01/admitting-you-were-wrong-doesnt-make-you-weak-it-makes-you-awesome/

http://www.leadergrow.com/articles/64-the-power-of-admitting-mistakes

Quote #7

"Quality is more important than quantity. One home run is much better than two doubles"

What did Jobs mean by this?

This is one of his most controversial quotes (not least because the analogy does not really work!) but it does make sense if you remove the fact his baseball knowledge is a little bit off!

The quote is trying to say that, for the most part, is that offering less quantity of sales for a higher quality of product that will have people coming back is more important than having a huge volume of sales that only see people come back once as it was not good enough. Making a quick buck is always possible, but it's always better to be remembered for the consistency and quality instead of anything else.

What did he do about it?

Well, he made sure Apple never produced cheaply made or auto-processed garbage. The ideology was always to be a technological leader instead of going along with the whole ideology of making lots of different products. Apple instead had a small grouping of products to sell that really were at the top of the quality ladder instead of selling lots of different, mediocre tools.

This is more important as having less selection but better output beats having lots of choice to pick from – but each choice is actually quite poor.

Why are you not doing this today?

Well, it's easy to see why a business may not follow this example. If you are in a busy marketplace it's easy to convince yourself that having more than one option for people to pick from is better than just the one selection they may not like/want. The problem with this is that spreading resources too thinly will hurt the overall productivity of the business massively and reduce the chances of being a success.

If you create less products of more quality you are likely to become a revered brand name with limited selection than a laughing stock with lots to pick from.

What can be learned from this?

Never take shortcuts with your offerings or products – in fact, never take shortcuts in life in general. Don't try and be a half-friend to lots, and instead concentrate on being a good friend to a few.

This is the same principle as with your own products that you see if you are in a business – it's all about treating people with respect and letting them show they know what they are looking for.

This is better than simple going along with the plan and making people feel like your products didn't fit as you tried too hard to please everyone. As Jobs worked on, create less but put more resources in and you are likely to succeed.

Resources to change for better

http://www.businessdictionary.com/article/581/the-importance-of-quality-over-quantity/

http://www.forbes.com/sites/jaysondemers/2014/10/20/quality-over-quantity-the-overblown-importance-of-likes-and-followers/

http://www.smartpassiveincome.com/the-truth-about-quantity-vs-quality/

Quote #8

"I think if you do something and it turns out pretty good, then you should go do something else wonderful, not dwell on it for too long. Just figure out what's next."

What he meant with it?

He knew that the creative process never stops. If you just dwell on your idea for too long you will:

- Missing out on creating something new, and to apply the creativity learned on the previous project on something new.

- Getting too obsessed with an idea that works, making difficult for you to change, vary or even innovate on it.

- Getting false a feeling of achievement, and create an image of success that is not everlasting.

- Dwell on your sense of security. It is your life. You have get our and seek new experiences and opportunities, never hide.

- Not being able to diversify your portfolio, and therefore the risks.

What did he do about it?

From the beginning he knew that innovation, design and staying ahead of the competition would be essential for success. Launching very rapidly different versions of iPads, and iPhones I was one of strategies. Also rectifying when he thought the design was not good enough (NEXT), to create NEXCube, and improved version.

Keeping patents during his way on the creative process was an habit as well.

Finally, integrating: Phones, computers, media players, music players, and internet. Anything he had invented already would be integrated into new devices: iPads and Iphones.

Why are you not doing this?

It sounds very pretentious from a genius like Steve Jobs to throw such a statement like the one above. It must be relatively easy to get one thing just right and then move on to do something else equally greatly, (or even better) when you are someone with such a creativity, intellect, and most importantly are surrounded by the elite in your industry.

Regular people struggle enough sometimes to find that idea, job, relationship, hobby or mastered skill that will make us feel better and safer. And when you are good at something, and got it precisely the way you wanted it, why should you try anything else? The answer is fear of failure.

The greater your successes, the greater the fear of failure.

What can you learn from it?

It is important sometimes in life to be honest with ourselves. What are we capable of? What is the stuff that prevent us from achieving more? We are not talking about of creating, but achieving something new, something refreshing that may make your life look brighter.

If there are financial of physical impediments, it is important to take note of them and to proceed accordingly. To draw a plan. A timeline.

Most of the times, however, such barriers will be in your mind, the psychological burden. We do not feel important. We are not great at this or that. These are the highest hurdles to jump sometimes, and the first step is to face them.

Once you have sorted the barriers that were once stopping you, a biggest issue comes right before you: To keep challenging yourself.

Resources to change for better

Here you will find clickable links to resources that will help you on moving forward in your life and never getting stuck in one thing:

1) For money management:

- https://www.mint.com
- https://www.youneedabudget.com
- https://www.gnucash.com
- https://infinitekind.com/moneydance
- https://www.budgetsimple.com

2) To find the root of your issues:

- http://www.anxietybc.com/sites/default/files/WorryScript.pdf
- http://www.anxietybc.com/adults/how-solve-daily-life-problems

  http://www.anxietybc.com/adults/how-tolerate-uncertainty

3) For when you run out of ideas:

- https://www.mindmeister.com/
- https://www.mindmeister.com/
- http://www.spiderscribe.net/
- http://www.xmind.net/

Printed in Great Britain
by Amazon